ISBN: 978-2-8399-3307-0

A LITTLE BOOK OF
REFLECTIONS
NEW INSIGHTS AND DISCOVERIES

Experiencing A New Way Of Living A Life After Covid – 19

Amyn Lalani

> **"If you love the life you live, you will live the life of love, joy and happiness. "**
>
> ~ Amyn Lalani

A Gift
of Inspiration
to All!

Image Courtesy: Faye Cornish | Composite Image: Deepta Dutta

Acknowledgements

"A Little Book Of Reflections: New Insights and Discoveries" is the product of many years of my curiosity that began as a child, when I was captivated by stars, planets and an enthusiasm that encouraged me to learn about the creation of this beauty in space.

As my journey moved me to Canada, I was researching and finding the answers to questions about my love for our beautiful universe. This in turn allowed me to find different tools and answers on my quest knowledge and this showed me the way to find the answers within.

I'd like to thank *Joanne Staradoum*, who introduced me to many different tools which helped me when I embarked on my journey, which I call a "**Journey of Transformative Education**."

Moving to Europe, I continued my commitment to this journey, although my life led me to a different education system, and I would like to thank the different schools that provided various opportunities to me. I extensively traveled the world and met many wonderful people, learnt about their amazing cultures, their values and I saw happiness in their eyes when making friends with their children, their parents and their families.

Thanks to *family and friends* who have supported me in new challenges that allowed me to settle into my new environment. This opened my desire to go deeper and find the truth for myself.

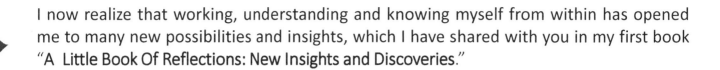

I now realize that working, understanding and knowing myself from within has opened me to many new possibilities and insights, which I have shared with you in my first book "A Little Book Of Reflections: New Insights and Discoveries."

My special thanks go to *Amarjyot Baidwan*, who committed to and understood my work and allowed the creation of this book while respecting, valuing and assisting me with the use of technology.

My deepest gratitude goes to *Deepta Dutta*, who spent valuable time on the illustration and design of the cover and text, with a wonderful selection of pictures that fit well with the different insights. In addition to this, Deepta helped me with self-publishing, and I truly appreciate her efforts.

My thanks also go to my freelance editor, *Matthew Ralph*, who has done a wonderful job of putting my words into perspective and he has given greater meaning to my work.

Finally, I would like to thank the *readers* of "The Little Book Of Reflections: Life after COVID-19." I have been gratified to hear the reader's responses and hope that your lives and your journeys take you to wonderful places of joy and happiness.

Introduction

It is quite amazing. The title of this little book came in my mind when I was thinking about my reflections of life during the COVID-19 crisis which the world is currently facing.

Why *reflections*? This refers to what humanity is experiencing in the world and has created this crisis, and how individuals can now learn a <u>new way of paying attention to life and motivate themselves so that the actions they take change their lives.</u>

This crisis then becomes and individual responsibility
<u>and a choice of the life they are living.</u>

So, this little book is about the reflections of life and learnings on <u>many new insights that I have discovered.</u> I want to share these practices with you to help people manage their stress, fears and many more individual crises.

I know this is difficult, and for many this is easier said than done. However, I have every intention of sharing these new insights with you all, so you can learn or practice these techniques and realize that the message from COVID-19 is also a message from the universe; it's a new way of looking at life.

Meanwhile, sit back, relax and enjoy reading the insights and lessons to learn!

Authors Notes

I have created a metaphor of a tree. The trunk of the tree is a solid red color, which represents your powerful strength. It also has several branches in green which represent different views of living life, from different insights that I have discovered, to sharing and briefly presenting a short explanations and illustrations which will bring a lot of peace, happiness, serenity and joy.

Most importantly, you will discover the truth about yourself, which will help bring more love into your life.

> **Love says "I am everything"... Wisdom says "I am nothing"...between the two my life flows**
>
> -Nisargadatta

TREE BRANCHES OF INSPIRATION

"*Life is a mystery to be lived, not a problem to be solved.*"

~ *Osho*

FIRST BRANCH:

View about Life

Image Courtesy: Łukasz Rawa | Composite Image: Deepta Dutta

Due to the COVID-19 crisis, your perspective and perception of life have been disrupted from you what you call your **normal, daily habitual routines and patterns, which you are used to.**

Many of you have strong habits that cannot change the patterns of your daily life, and many people are reflecting on the many new ways their lives are changing. These people are also asking **what has happened to the world around us.**

Well, many of you who are going through different experiences, have discovered or perhaps not discovered that this has been put into reality or illusion in the world for each one of us **to awaken and understand the different possibilities of living.**

What I am talking about is that many of you have strong, patterned personalities filled with the ego of your habits and fixations. So, the main key factors affecting people emotionally and mentally during this time are:

FEAR & LONELINESS.

what covid-19 is showing us is that there is more to humanity and life than just living a life of fear, stress, old habits and loneliness.

Change

> **It's how we spend our time here and now, that really matters. If you are fed up with the way you have come to interact with time, change it.**
>
> ~ Marcia Wieder

All truths are easy to understand once they are discovered; the point is to discover them.

~ Galileo Galilei

So , the insights I discovered, they bring to your attention, living a life of truth - your real self which is authentic, real and can change and experience a proper life with truth and staying in the moment. This helps to develop more power and strength just like the trunk of the tree. The true objective of life is to discover love within you.

Why do individuals hide the truth in the way they communicate and do individuals hide the truth in the way they communicate and in their daily work lives? Because traditionally you are told that the truth hurts. In many ways we do not act based to the truth. We act based on the truth we believe. In your view of life, if you were to even consider being truthful to yourself and to others, this would bring about a different feeling inside of you- **a feeling of change.**

EXAMPLE 1

Your mind thinks you don't have money. Now, is it true that you don't have any money at all? Look in your pocket; you probably have at least a penny.

So, yes, the truth is you do have money and you should thank yourself that you have that penny. When you do this kind of exercise, think about what happens to your mind. You are telling truth.

The truth brings lots of change inside you in your day-to-day life.

"It is health that is real wealth and not pieces of gold and silver."

~ Mahatma Gandhi

EXAMPLE 2

You are afraid of COVID-19. Yes, it is true you are afraid. It is the truth that you are afraid. The truth is also that you are healthy and most likely do not have COVID-19. Now, where should you focus your attention? Pay attention to the truth that you are healthy and thank yourself. Then see what happens to the energy in yourself.

For those who become infected with COVID-19 – the truth is that you are alive, and you should be thankful that. Put your attention on the things that bring more positive feelings to your life, thing things that are true about yourself and you will recognize how you feel inside.

So, the first insight is learning, practicing the view of living your life with truth and tell yourself this is the truth. Slowly practice with different things and you will discover a change happening in yourself.

When I say, "live authentically", this means to be fully, genuine to yourselves and understand your inner flow within you as well as external activities, and you will begin loving yourself more.

So, the Insights of the 1st Branch of the Tree Suggest:

Insight #1 - Being Authentic:

Just telling simple truths to yourself and expanding this in many areas of your daily routines will bring change to your life. There will be feelings on oneness inside you and you may discover more strength that will be derived from within you. You will start respecting yourself more.

Insight #2 - Clarity on Reflections of Your Life:

Focus your attention on your ability to identify what you really love in your life and what you really want so you can get out of it. Don't let fear stop you because when you channel your fears, they will give you an opportunity to grow and be successful. So, deal with your stress, doubts, and the barriers to success, as these are opportunities for growth. These reflections also help you to examine your real motivations and once you have discovered those motivations, you will take precise action. You will have a different mental image of yourself.

Insight #3 - Living in the Moment:

It is easy to see that we can only be happy in the moment, so enjoy every moment as each moment brings new learnings. Remember nothing exists outside of the here and now.

Insight #4 - Developing Trust:

You will develop trust in yourself when you tell truth. When you build trust in yourself, you will discover more strength with integrity, so it is a matter of changing your character so you can enjoy your communication with others. In addition to this, trust will bring other qualities within yourself such as power and authority.

Insight #5 - Discovering Yourself:

When you discover yourself out of box by telling truth, you will be surprised how much laughter you have that will stimulate you. Even when you feel pain, and when you change the projection of your mind, you see a life full of laughter, joy and peace. You will discover more of yourself. Then, you will lift yourself to a new level and will be able to show others how to lift themselves up too.

Many of you, I feel, are thinking that habitual patterns are difficult to break, which is why people are fighting to go back to work.

The real question is what is more essential: your health or work?

How can you balance these two areas of life?

This is an opening to the insights that each one of you is there to prepare and learn that there is more to life than just your fixations of daily routine. Many of you have had lessons in yoga, exercise and spent time discovering how to be at peace, so you started meditation.

What did all these messages give you?

Start living a life of truth and it can bring new changes, happiness and new dreams to your life!

SECOND BRANCH:

Living in Abundance

What people also realize is that many of them have experienced different crises in life, such as financial loss, job loss, business loss or loss of income. Many people are so attached to these ways of living. Yes, it is sad to go through this and that is why there are lessons to learn from different perspectives of living your life.

People are not accustomed to sudden changes in life, so they start to experience fear and many other negative emotions follow. It is like an earthquake or a tsunami, where people lose everything in just one night.

Here, people realize that there is a battle between humanity and the economy, instead of seeing *real* truth of health in humanity and the economy. This is due to the unknown amount of information in this new pandemic, and on top of that, the ignorance and panic among follows as people struggle with how to cope with this.

So, this is how I suggest you can inspire yourself and live in any life situation.

What COVID-19 has taught us is that love, laughter and happiness come from developing your inner talents. So, when a situation like this happens, people develop their consciousness to a new level and can accept their ability to change and master their circumstances. That is why so much valuable information is out there about acknowledging different exercise methods, breathing exercises, meditation and much more.

These methods have probably at least brought in temporary peace to your life at that moment but probably did not bring a total solution.

26

1st Insight: Feeling Secure

Insecurity in life comes from worries, doubts, fears and many more areas. This is what many people are taught to believe inside them. But it is also true that **security** comes from within yourself when you change your mind patterns and when you believe in yourself, you are control of your mind.

"Life is full and overflowing with the new. But it is also necessary to empty out the old to make room for the new to enter."
~ Eileen Caddy

2nd Insight: Feeling Abundance

You know when you are healthy, you feel fully functional in society. Therefore, many people discover, through many different channels, that when you start living a life of truth, from a true self point of view, it means loving yourself more and stop anxiety. Don't give in to worries and doubts (the old patterns of insecurity). You will soon realize it changes you and you can start living a life of abundance.

What does abundance mean? One of the first things that come to mind is money and that is true. You need money, but real abundance is when you live a life of truth, self-love, instead of you allowing your old patterns to control your life. You need to understand yourself and feel that every aspect of life is valuable to you. You can sincerely enjoy love, laughter and happiness, and money, abundance and wealth are the reward of these.

"You will feel like a failure until you impress the subconscious with the conviction you are a success. This is done by making an affirmation which clicks."

~ Florence Scovel Shinn

3rd Insight: True Self Esteem

How you evaluate yourself and judge your own self and having a valued opinion of yourself makes a big difference in your life. This can bring lots of confidence, courage so you can value yourself. People are very sensitive about their sense of worth and are interested in making a good impression about them to others. Therefore, deep down, they feel insecure because they are finding or looking for value from outside sources and this brings a deep sense of low self-esteem. So, feeling and finding your true self-esteem will bring you to a level of your real intrinsic value about yourself, and you will therefore feel abundant and secure.

"The universe has billions of ways to keep us humble and fascinated all at the same time."

Mike Pearson

4th Insight: Being Responsible and Freedom of Living:

Responsibility with a choice opens many possibilities in life. Letting go of your old habits and patterns is not easy. People go through lots of suffering in the process of trying to free themselves from pain. The insight here is to discover and understand that there are other ways of looking at life than just being attached to old beliefs patterns. Every moment in life has lots of possibilities when you love yourself. Our lives change when our behavior changes to open up to and be responsible for new freedom.

❝Liberation is not very far away; it is just hidden behind you. Once you are authentic the door opens. We can be such liars, pretenders, hypocrites, so deeply false, that's why we feel liberation is very far away. It is not! For an authentic being, liberation is just natural as anything.❞

~Osho

THIRD BRANCH:

Living in Relationships and Social Interactions

Creating Harmony

Image Composite: Deepta Dutta

If you look at your life during this pandemic, many of you have been separated from children, grandparents and boyfriend and girlfriend etc. And, yes, you went through a period of inner tension and crisis which was beyond your expectations.

This area created the biggest tensions: worries, fear, stress and loneliness for many people. Thanks to social media and technology, you can constantly stay in touch with each other. Although what you discovered that there is a different feeling when you are separated– even if technology works, it is still not the same as real human interaction.

The insight to discover here is that each one of us has a relationship that has feelings and thoughts that you can only feel with real human contact. When working together and everything is close to each other, there is trust, caring and love.

You are too accustomed in your life to ignoring that truth mentioned above, because you are always living a life of ego, have a personality of selfishness or are running away from relationships. Think about it, more people long for love during the Christmas period and so many more people want love more on St Valentine's Day, rather than all year round.

Loving <u>yourself</u> is the Most Important thing!

The various *insights* to discover here are that during this time the world, each country has started taking care of themselves and working to develop relationships, helping people who are sick, there are lots of volunteers around, lots of sacrifices and a lot of generosity.

1st Insight: Strength and Character:

Your strength and character come from your inner self. It comes from your different beliefs and the choices you make. However, your real character is built from your self-esteem. So many of those who were able to be calm during the pandemic probably recognized their inner strength, their character and many of their ideals about the choices they made and can face these challenges. But those who are going into new challenges need to investigate these areas and overcome their limitations.

"People do not lack strength, they lack will."

~ Victor Hugo

2nd Insight: Loving Yourself:

What this insight brings about is being gentle to yourself, the ability to be close to your own self and having a healthy relationship within your emotions. This will give you an opportunity to be able to augment your relationships in life. There is a lot written about the importance of intimacy and caring.

Take all the time you need to heal emotionally.
Heal at your own pace. Step by step. Day by day.
~ Karen Salmansohn

3rd Insight: Being Fulfilled and Being Happy:

Regardless of your relationship, career or the life you live, it is essential to reach the stage where you feel happy and fulfilled within yourself and then your relationships will improve. Deep down in every heart, there a is great longing for happiness. Enjoy and develop your true passion; relax and meditate and stay focused. The journey of life will be fun. Take time to bond with your loved ones all year-round; your life is happening in the now. You should be your own star and look at the many benefits and strength you bring. Enjoy the little things too and outside nature brings beauty and happiness.

If you are locked down, look at beautiful pictures of nature and that will bring a smile to your face, or read something valuable that brings new understanding to your life. Remember the desire of happiness is good and you will realize this within yourself, and this then leads us to expanding our horizons.

"*Happiness is your nature. It is not wrong to desire it. What is wrong is seeking it outside when it is inside.*" Ramana Maharshi

4th Insight: Taking Action to Renew Yourself:

One of the key ingredients that helps build your relationship is having a positive attitude and developing positive thinking. Thoughts are energy, so immerse in thoughts of kindness, gratitude, love, the potential of life, life goals and more.

To renew yourself means re-aligning yourself to your beliefs, your thought patterns and your emotions, which have a clear focus about your dreams. Be a self-motivated person, empathetic, show optimism, understanding relationships and most importantly, become self-aware.

"The more honest and authentic we are, the more deeply we go into the mystery of our own being."

~ Adyashanti

FOURTH BRANCH:

Living a life of Health and Wellness

Here again, the old patterns of life show that many people who are daily gym goers and do physical exercise are strained by that and have therefore built tension and confusion, which leads to fighting within themselves.

You can understand that health and wellness have been the key to your functioning in life and sometimes your physical body gets tired, and you are pushed to the limits and create pain in your body.

This pandemic has taught us many life lessons, such as during this time many professionals, such as gym instructors or personal trainers have discovered new ways of creating our own workouts and of course, technology helps us with this.

Again, the personality and your structure of patterns are focused on your body and mind. Many of you have become like machines who continue to cycle and continue to fitness. However, there is nothing wrong with doing those exercises. The insights that COVID-19 is giving us is that you need a well-balanced life, which means that you are either too mentally focused or too emotionally charged up.

You require balance in both the emotional and mental side of your body, which brings balance to you inside so you can reap the benefits.

1st Insight: Emotional Openness:

All your inspiration comes from yourself within from your true self. Humans are not only made ill by his/her negative thoughts, but also emotions that are not processed. Thoughts can be controlled and reversed instead of repressing them.

Once you feel those thoughts that have patterned your mind, feel them completely. You will release lots of negative energy and bring in lots of transformative thoughts, which will also affect your body and life around you. Once you learn to handle your thoughts and feelings, you will understand that you have lots of peace within you and the world around you.

Love people for who they are, not for who you want them to be.

2nd Insight: Expand Your Consciousness:

Let your consciousness expand by allowing yourself to expand through meditation, yoga and most importantly, through learning about life and living a life of truth. This insight is essential because it helps each and every individual to learn how to process a life of false beliefs.

Release the emotions that you were falsely taught, then you will slowly start to discover the real power you hold within. There is infinite supply of power around you; all you need to know is how to draw on it and how to use in your daily life.

To be able to give and receive love,
you first need to know who you are.

3rd Insight : Allow For Healthy Living:

One of the key essentials to a person's health is regular exercise; even light exercise brings your consciousness fulfillment. Every day establish a schedule to do exercise to strengthen your body.

However, you are not limited to gym, so allow yourself to do something that you enjoy doing, something to suit your lifestyle and what you prefer. Exercise brings a positive mental impact on individuals.

If you don't make the time for exercise, you'll probably have to make time for illness.

~ Robin Sharma

4th Insight: Enhancing Your Wellness:

Wellness is about enhancing your body overall. Many of you have established these routines during COVID-19, however it is essential to have a good sleep, practice meditation, yoga and deep breathing exercises.

All this help you to lower your anxiety, depression or any negative thoughts. The journey of life is to enjoy the things that bring positive results.

> **Health is a state of complete harmony of the body, mind and spirit.**
>
> ~ B.K.S. Iyengar

Additional Insights:

The other insights came to me as information to share certain qualities and when you look closely inside you, many of you will discover that you already have **charisma, courage, commitment, respect, compassion, integrity,** and a lot more.

FINAL THOUGHTS

It was interesting that everyone started clapping at night as a way of thanking and appreciating the front-line workers and many volunteers helping those in need. I hope the world changes with more peace and harmony from the lessons we are all learning from COVID-19.

And these are the insights that I personally discovered and want to share them. I hope that it opens you to love, even when you are separated from people. This is the beginning of looking into and opening yourself up to this information in the form of insights and realize how they have helped you survive through many challenges. Many of you are aware of these insights and therefore knew how to cope with the pandemic. I sincerely hope for those who find this information useful, you will benefit from this, have courage to survive and continue living a new way of life so that we all can bring conscious expansion to the world. Humanity needs to be taken care of like one big family and we need to let go of all our differences.

Yes, the world went into darkness and is coming out slowly and we need to start focusing on these new insights and integrate old habits to these new ones. This will allow a new way of life, with joy, laughter, wellbeing and happiness.

Thank you for reading my book, A Little Book of Reflections, and I hope these insights have given you hope to discover yourself & move forward.

You must go into darkness to come out at the light so that you can enjoy happiness and live a life of joy and value your life.   ~ Amyn Lalani

With love and happiness.

Image Courtesy: Siyaa Moni Gulati

About the Author

Amyn is a teacher, advisor and a mentor on transformative education based in Switzerland and written his first book on life`s reflection after covid-19. His own transformational journey has spanned over 3 continents - Africa, Europe & North America and where he has been learning the truth and finding the answers of life for himself. He has completely devoted himself to help transform the lives of his clients through simple techniques of self-reflection and mindfulness.

He has travelled extensively around Central and Eastern Asia, the Middle East as well as Western and Eastern Europe, North America to develop business schools achieve several strategic plans and objectives.

In addition to this, Amyn has over 18 years of corporate experience with various multinationals in Canada where he managed end-to-end projects, which means he understands all functional activities and what it takes to effectively and efficiently increase performance and achieve results.

Amyn is the owner and founder of "Starship Management and Services", an organization which provides excellence in knowledge management and gives people the tools needed to make a difference in their organizational performance and effectiveness in their personal lives. He has now created a new personal development and transformative education system called the "Transformative Education". The academy provides human understanding to develop and expand a client's potential in both their professional and personal lives.

Amyn holds regular Q&A sessions for clients and is available for on-line versions of specific workshops.

"This crisis then becomes an individual responsibility and a choice of living their life."

Amyn Lalani

For more information about joining one of his programs or to find out more information, visit Amyn's blog: www.transformative-education.com

CPSIA information can be obtained
at www.ICGtesting.com
Printed in the USA
LVHW072221030921
696802LV00018B/27